SOLIDWORKS Exercises
Learn by Practicing
Design 50 Real-World 3D Models by Practicing

CADArtifex

The premium provider of learning products and solutions
www.cadartifex.com

SOLIDWORKS Exercises: Learn by Practicing

Published by
CADArtifex
www.cadartifex.com

ISBN-13: 978-1548361280
ISBN-10: 1548361283

NOTICE TO THE READER
The publisher and the author make no representations or warranties with respect to the accuracy or completeness of the contents of this work/text and specifically disclaim all warranties, including without limitation warranties of fitness for a particular purpose. Publisher does not guarantee any of the products described in the text or perform any independent analysis in connection with any of the product information contained in the text. No warranty may be created or extended by sales or promotional materials. This work is sold with the understanding that the publisher is not engaged in rendering legal, accounting, or other professional services. Neither the publisher nor the author shall be liable for damages arising herefrom. Further, readers should be aware that Internet Websites listed in this work may have changed or disappeared between when this work was written and when it is read.

Examination Copies
Books received as examination copies in any form such as paperback and eBook are for review only and may not be made available for the use of the student. These files may not be transferred to any other party. Resale of examination copies is prohibited.

Electronic Files
The electronic file/eBook in any form of this book is licensed to the original user only and may not be transferred to any other party.

Disclaimer
The author has made sincere efforts to ensure the accuracy of the material described herein, however the author makes no warranty, expressed or implied, with respect to the quality, correctness, accuracy, or freedom from error of this document or the products it describes.

www.cadartifex.com

Dedication

First and foremost, I would like to thank my parents for being a great support throughout my career and while writing this book.

Heartfelt thanks go to all the users of *SOLIDWORKS 2017: A Power Guide for Beginners and Intermediate Users* textbook published by **CADArtifex** for inspiring me in taking this challenge.

I would also like to acknowledge the efforts of the employees at CADArtifex for their dedication in editing the content of this book.

Table of Contents

Preface

SOLIDWORKS, developed by Dassault Systèmes SOLIDWORKS Corp., one of the biggest technology providers to engineering, offers complete 3D software tools that let you create, simulate, publish, and manage data. The products of SOLIDWORKS are easy to learn and use, and are integrated with each other to help you design products accurately, fast, and cost-effectively.

SOLIDWORKS delivers a rich set of integrated tools that are powerful and intuitive to use. It is a feature-based, parametric solid-modeling mechanical design, and automation software that allows you to create real-world 3D components and assemblies by using simple but highly effective tools. The 3D components and assemblies created in SOLIDWORKS can be converted into 2D drawings with few mouse clicks. In addition, you can validate your designs by simulating their real-world conditions and assess the environmental impact of your products.

SOLIDWORKS Exercises: Learn by Practicing book is designed to help engineers and designers interested in learning SOLIDWORKS by practicing 50 real-world mechanical models. This book does not provide step-by-step instructions to design 3D models. Instead, its a practice book that challenges users to first analyze the drawings and then create the models using the powerful toolset of SOLIDWORKS. This approach helps users to enhance their design skills and take it to the next level. You can download all exercises used in this book for free by logging into our website (*www.cadartifex.com*).

Who Should Read This Book

This book is written with a wide range of SOLIDWORKS users in mind, varying from beginners to advanced users. In addition to SOLIDWORKS, each exercise of this book can also be designed on any other CAD software such as Catia, Creo Parametric, NX, Autodesk Inventor, and Solid Edge.

Prerequisites

To complete the exercises given in this book, you should have knowledge of SOLIDWORKS. If you want to learn SOLIDWORKS step-by-step, you can refer to the *SOLIDWORKS 2017: A Power Guide for Beginners and Intermediate Users* textbook published by CADArtifex.

What Is Covered in This Book

SOLIDWORKS Exercises: Learn by Practicing book consists of 50 real-world mechanical models. After creating these models, you would be able to take your design skills to the professional level.

Download

The exercises used in this book are available for free download. To download the exercises, follow the steps given below:

1. Login to the **CADArtifex** website (*www.cadartifex.com*) by using your username and password. If you are new user, you need first to register on **CADArtifex** website as a student.

2. After login to the **CADArtifex** website, click on SOLIDWORKS > SOLIDWORKS Exercises. Now, you can download the exercises of this book by using the **Exercises** drop-down list.

How to Contact the Author

We always value the feedback we receive from our readers. If you have any suggestions or feedback, please write to us at *info@cadartifex.com*. You can also provide your feedback by logging into our webiste *www.cadartifex.com*.

Thank you very much for purchasing *SOLIDWORKS Exercises: Learn by Practicing* book, we hope that the exercises given in this book will help you to accomplish your professional goals.

SOLIDWORKS Exercises: Learn by Practicing

Each of the 50 exercises of the book can be designed separately. No exercise is a prerequisite for another. All the dimensions used in the exercises are in **mm**. The drawing views of the exercises given in this book follow the third angle of projection. In the third angle of projection, the projection of the front view of the model appears on the bottom and the projection of the top view appears on the top in the drawing. Also, the right side view appears on the right and the left side view appears on the left of the front view.

Exercise 1.

Create the 3D model shown in Figure 1. Different views of the model and dimensions are shown in Figure 2. All dimensions are in **mm**.   [Expected time: 20 min]

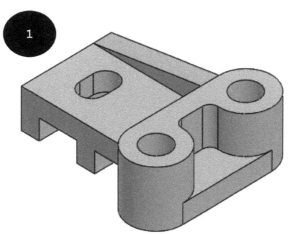

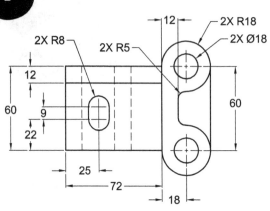

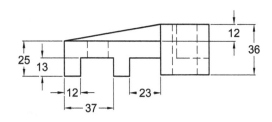

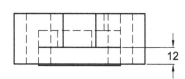

Exercise 2.

Create the 3D model shown in Figure 3. Different views of the model and dimensions are shown in Figure 4. All dimensions are in **mm**. [Expected time: 20 min]

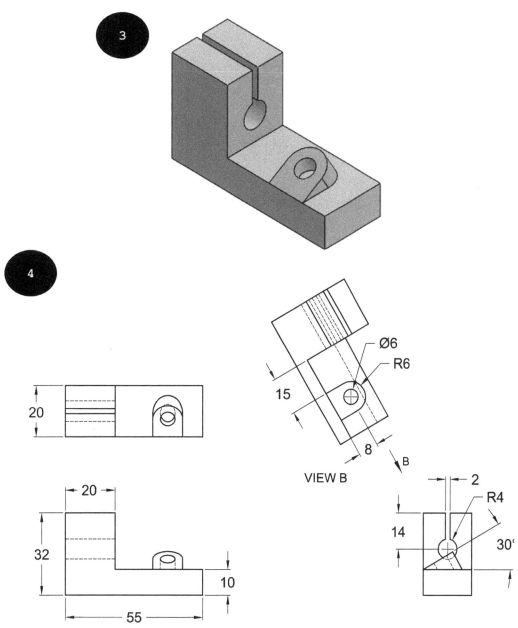

Exercise 3.

Create the 3D model shown in Figure 5. Different views of the model and dimensions are shown in Figure 6. All dimensions are in **mm**.   [Expected time: 20 min]

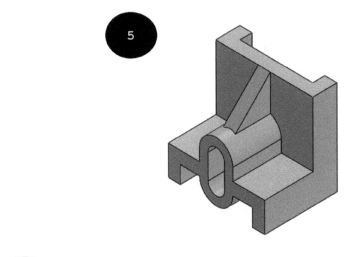

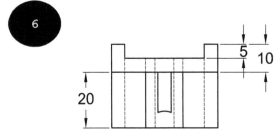

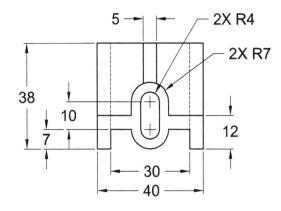

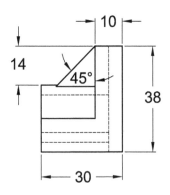

Exercise 4.

Create the 3D model shown in Figure 7. Different views of the model and dimensions are shown in Figure 8. All dimensions are in **mm**. [Expected time: 20 min]

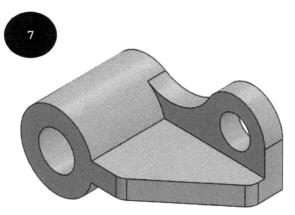

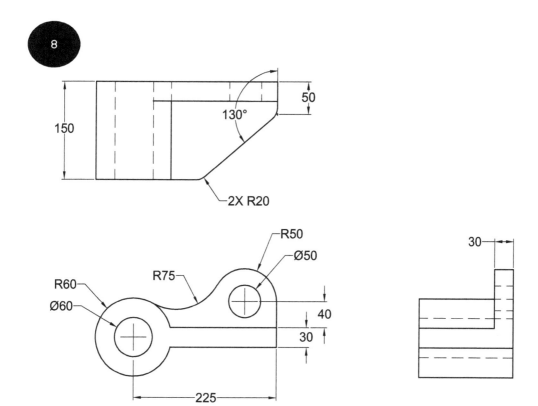

Exercise 5.

Create the 3D model shown in Figure 9. Different views of the model and dimensions are shown in Figure 10. All dimensions are in **mm**. [Expected time: 20 min]

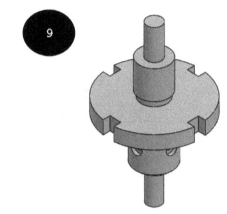

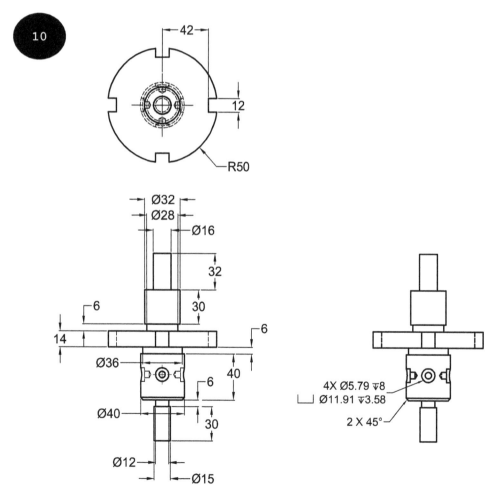

Exercise 6.

Create the 3D model shown in Figure 11. Different views of the model and dimensions are shown in Figure 12. All dimensions are in **mm**.　　　　　　　　　　　　　　　　[Expected time: 25 min]

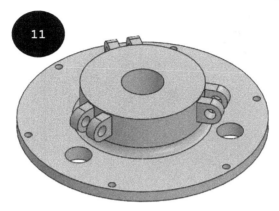

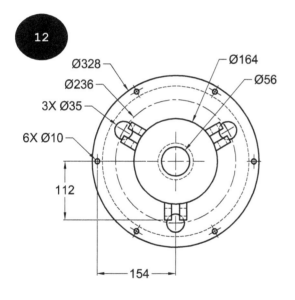

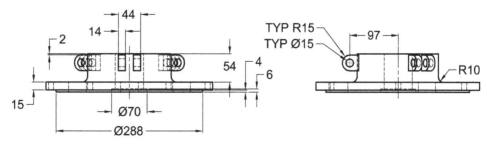

Exercise 7.

Create the 3D model shown in Figure 13. Different views of the model and dimensions are shown in Figure 14. All dimensions are in **mm**.   [Expected time: 25 min]

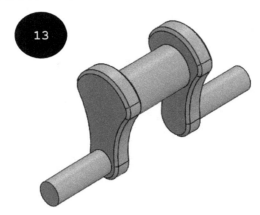

13

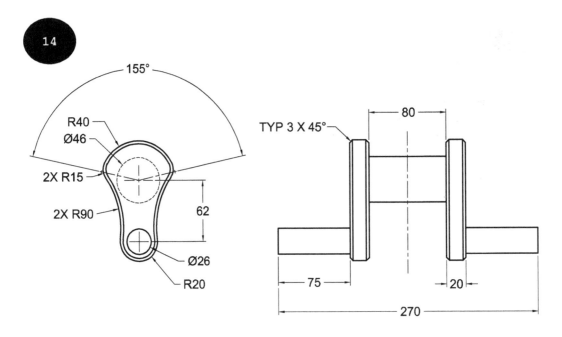

14

155°

R40
Ø46

2X R15

2X R90

62

Ø26

R20

TYP 3 X 45°

80

75

20

270

Exercise 8.

Create the 3D model shown in Figure 15. Different views of the model and dimensions are shown in Figure 16. All dimensions are in **mm**. [Expected time: 20 min]

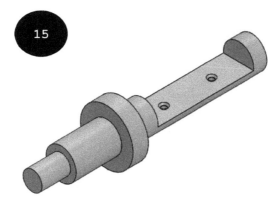

15

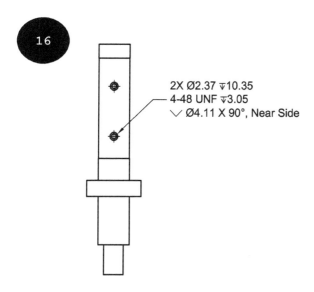

16

2X Ø2.37 ⩒10.35
4-48 UNF ⩒3.05
∨ Ø4.11 X 90°, Near Side

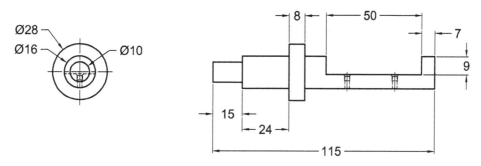

Ø28
Ø16
Ø10

8
50
7
9
15
24
115

Exercise 9.

Create the 3D model shown in Figure 17. Different views of the model and dimensions are shown in Figure 18. All dimensions are in **mm**. [Expected time: 25 min]

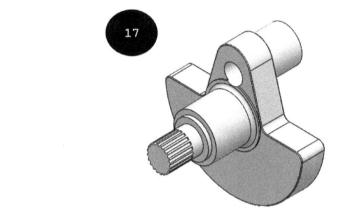

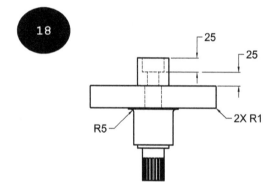

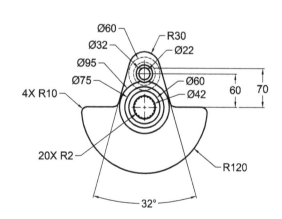

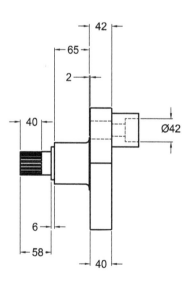

Exercise 10.

Create the 3D model shown in Figure 19. Different views of the model and dimensions are shown in Figure 20. All dimensions are in **mm**.   [Expected time: 25 min]

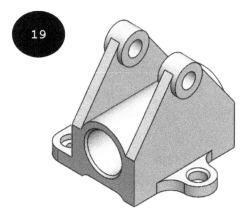

19

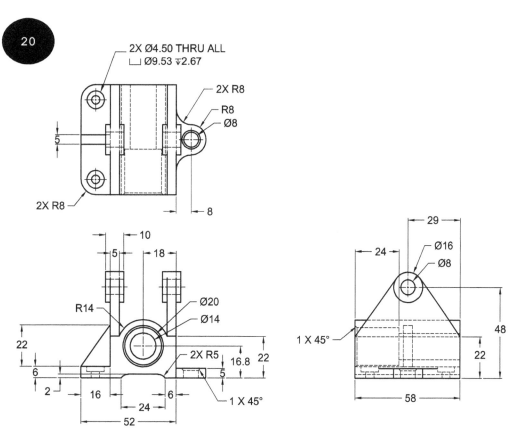

20

Exercise 11.

Create the 3D model shown in Figure 21. Different views of the model and dimensions are shown in Figure 22. All dimensions are in **mm**. [Expected time: 25 min]

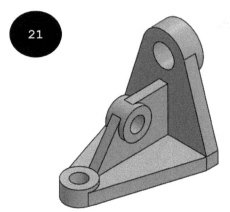

21

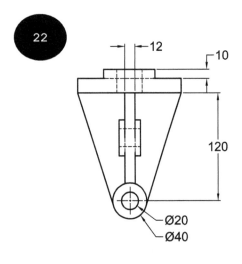

22

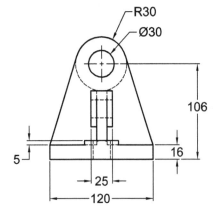

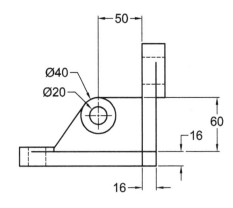

Exercise 12.

Create the 3D model shown in Figure 23. Different views of the model and dimensions are shown in Figure 24. All dimensions are in **mm**. [Expected time: 30 min]

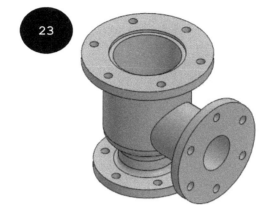

23

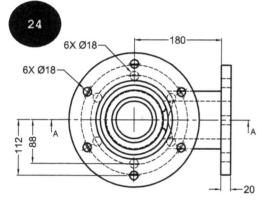

24

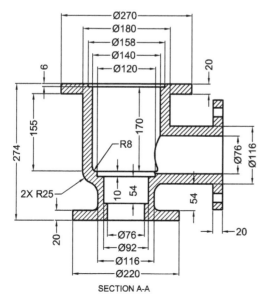

SECTION A-A

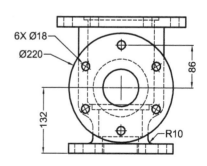

Exercise 13.

Create the 3D model shown in Figure 25. Different views of the model and dimensions are shown in Figure 26. All dimensions are in **mm**.   [Expected time: 25 min]

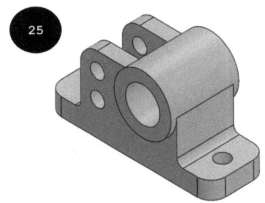

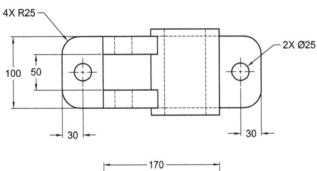

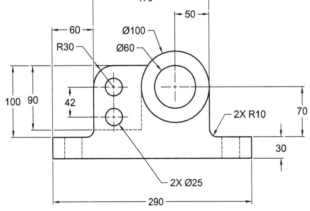

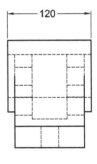

Exercise 14.

Create the 3D model shown in Figure 27. Different views of the model and dimensions are shown in Figure 28. All dimensions are in **mm**.   [Expected time: 35 min]

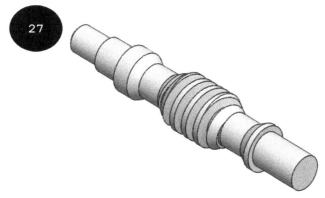

27

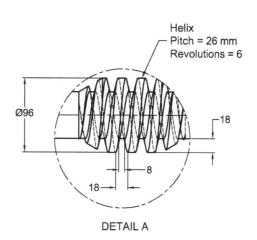

28

Helix
Pitch = 26 mm
Revolutions = 6

Ø96

18

8

18

DETAIL A

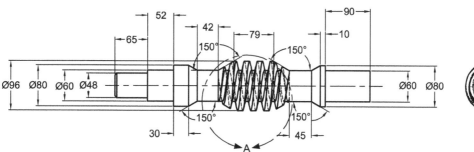

52

42

79

90

65

150°

10

150°

Ø96 Ø80 Ø60 Ø48

150°

150°

Ø60 Ø80

30

150°

150°

45

A

Exercise 15.

Create the 3D model shown in Figure 29. Different views of the model and dimensions are shown in Figure 30. All dimensions are in **mm**. [Expected time: 15 min]

29

30

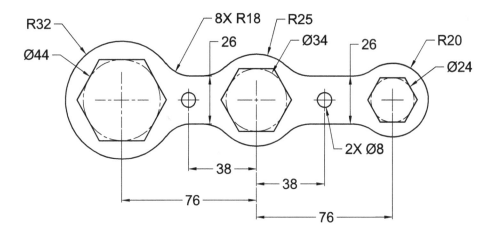

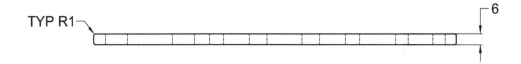

Exercise 16.

Create the 3D model shown in Figure 31. Different views of the model and dimensions are shown in Figure 32. All dimensions are in **mm**. [Expected time: 30 min]

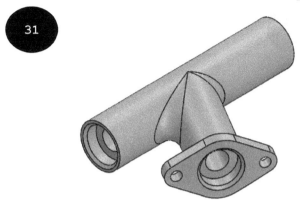

31

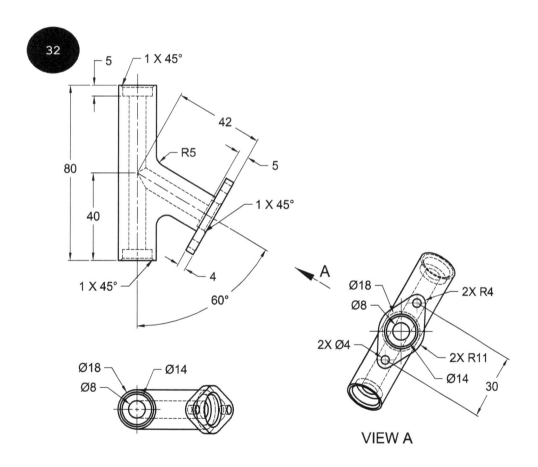

32

5   1 X 45°

42

R5

80

5

40

1 X 45°

4

60°

1 X 45°

Ø18   Ø14

Ø8

A

Ø18   2X R4

Ø8

2X Ø4

2X R11

Ø14   30

VIEW A

Exercise 17.

Create the 3D model shown in Figure 33. Different views of the model and dimensions are shown in Figure 34. All dimensions are in **mm**.   [Expected time: 25 min]

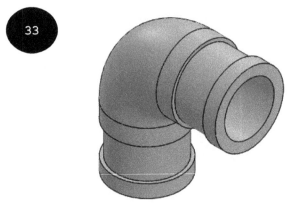

33

34

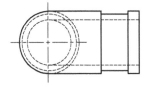

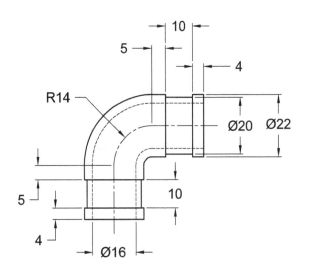

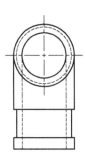

Exercise 18.

Create the 3D model shown in Figure 35. Different views of the model and dimensions are shown in Figure 36. All dimensions are in **mm**. [Expected time: 35 min]

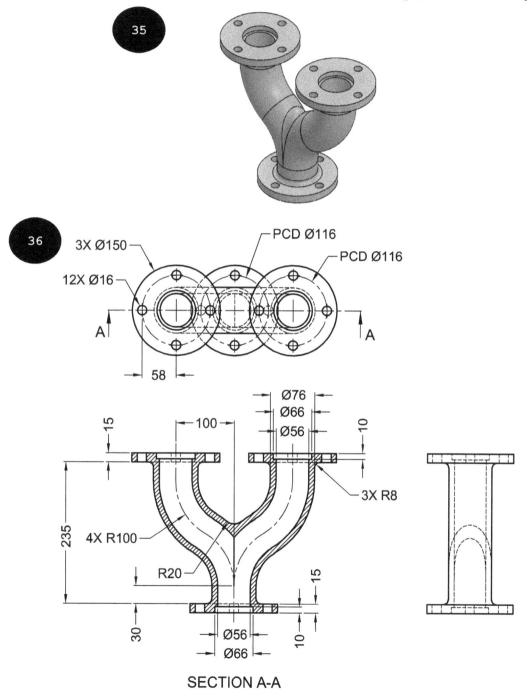

Exercise 19.

Create the 3D model shown in Figure 37. Different views of the model and dimensions are shown in Figure 38. All dimensions are in **mm**.   [Expected time: 35 min]

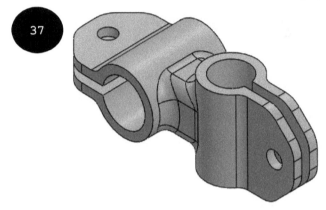

37

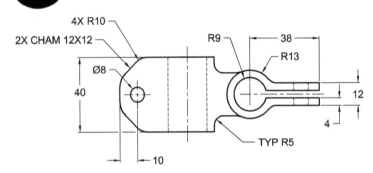

38

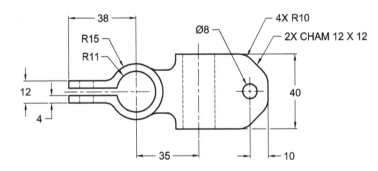

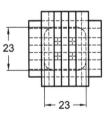

Exercise 20.

Create the 3D model shown in Figure 39. Different views of the model and dimensions are shown in Figure 40. All dimensions are in **mm**. [Expected time: 30 min]

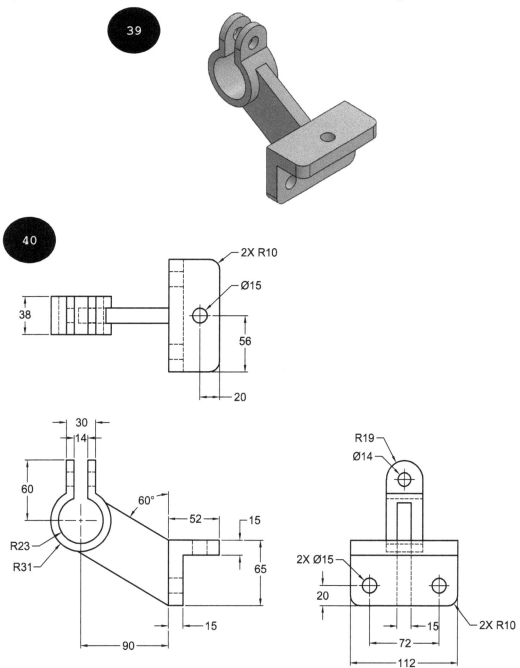

Exercise 21.

Create the 3D model shown in Figure 41. Different views of the model and dimensions are shown in Figure 42. All dimensions are in **mm**. [Expected time: 30 min]

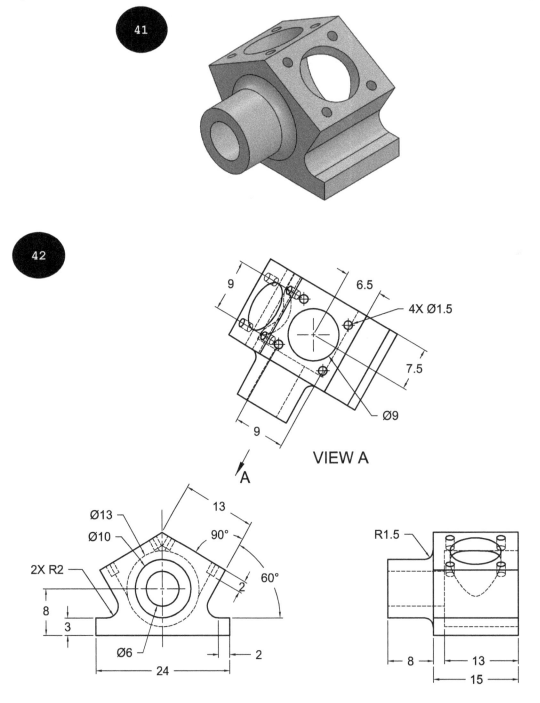

Exercise 22.

Create the 3D model shown in Figure 43. Different views of the model and dimensions are shown in Figure 44. All dimensions are in **mm**. [Expected time: 30 min]

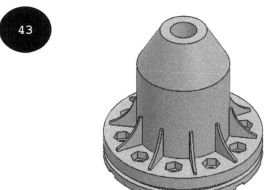

43

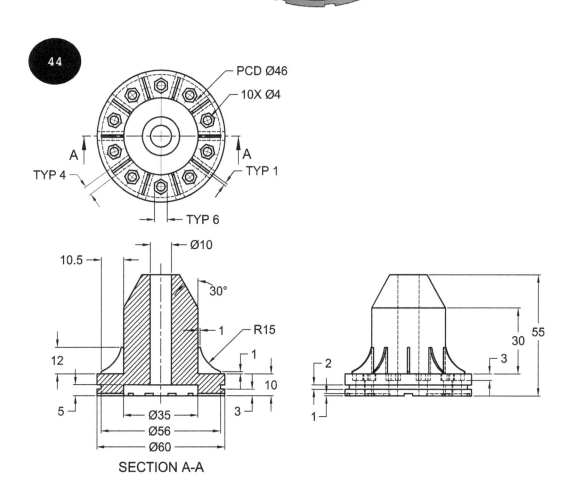

44

PCD Ø46

10X Ø4

A

A

TYP 4

TYP 1

TYP 6

Ø10

10.5

30°

1 — R15

12

1

10

5

Ø35

3

Ø56

Ø60

55

30

2

3

1

SECTION A-A

Exercise 23.

Create the 3D model shown in Figure 45. Different views of the model and dimensions are shown in Figure 46. All dimensions are in **mm**.   [Expected time: 30 min]

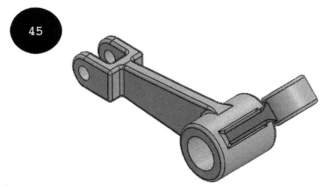

45

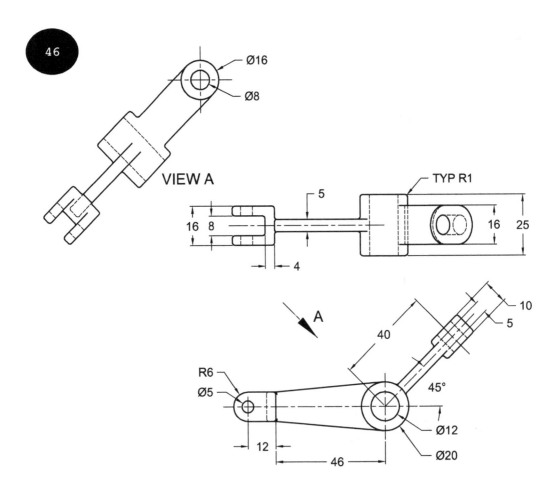

46

Exercise 24.

Create the 3D model shown in Figure 47. Different views of the model and dimensions are shown in Figure 48. All dimensions are in **mm**.   [Expected time: 30 min]

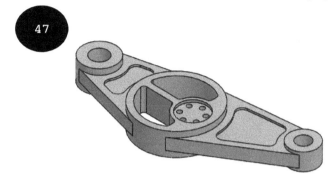

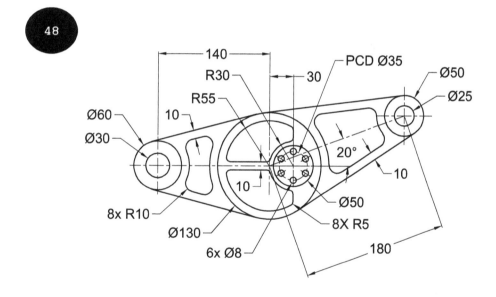

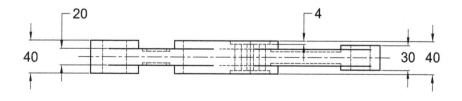

Exercise 25.

Create the 3D model shown in Figure 49. Different views of the model and dimensions are shown in Figure 50. All dimensions are in **mm**.   [Expected time: 30 min]

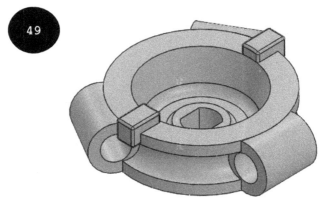

49

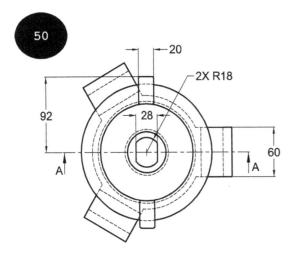

50

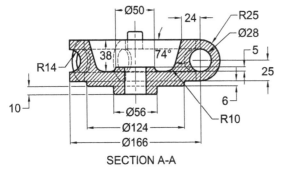

SECTION A-A

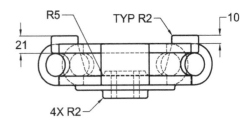

Exercise 26.

Create the 3D model shown in Figure 51. Different views of the model and dimensions are shown in Figure 52. All dimensions are in **mm**. [Expected time: 25 min]

51

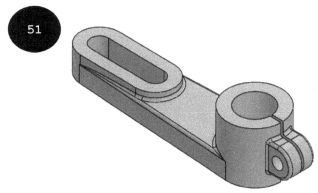

52

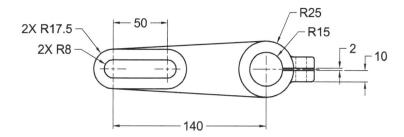

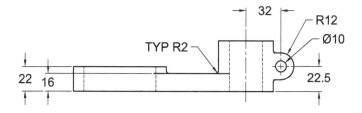

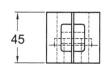

Exercise 27.

Create the 3D model shown in Figure 53. Different views of the model and dimensions are shown in Figure 54. All dimensions are in **mm**.   [Expected time: 25 min]

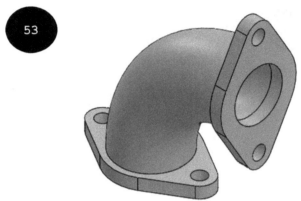

53

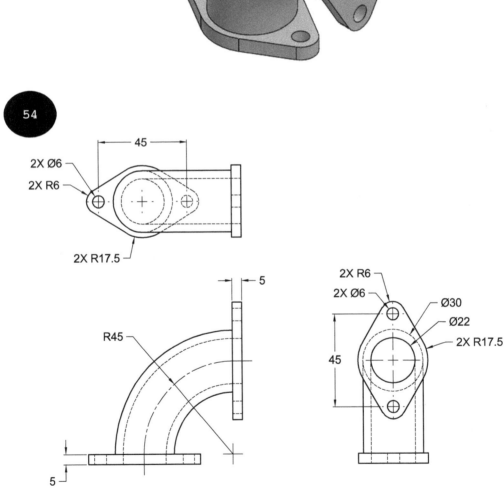

54

Exercise 28.

Create the 3D model shown in Figure 55. Different views of the model and dimensions are shown in Figure 56. All dimensions are in **mm**.   [Expected time: 30 min]

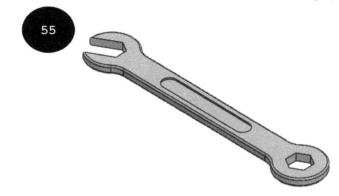

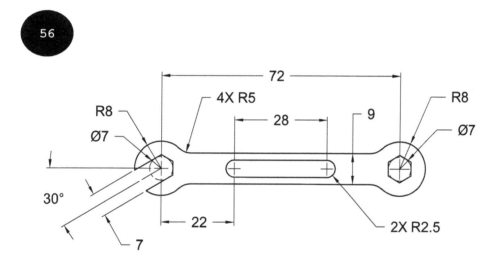

Exercise 29.

Create the 3D model shown in Figure 57. Different views of the model and dimensions are shown in Figure 58. All dimensions are in **mm**.   [Expected time: 25 min]

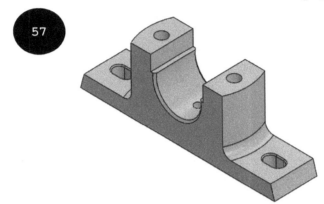

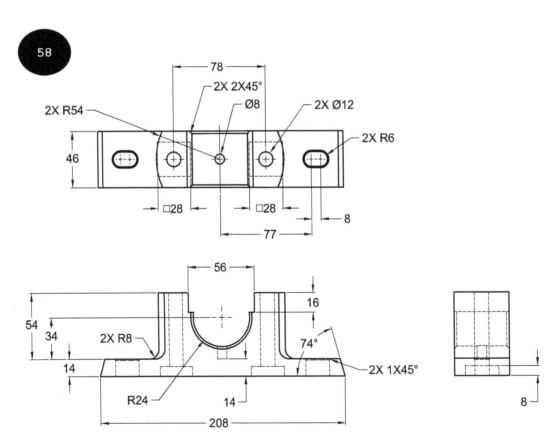

Exercise 30.

Create the 3D model shown in Figure 59. Different views of the model and dimensions are shown in Figure 60. All dimensions are in **mm**. [Expected time: 40 min]

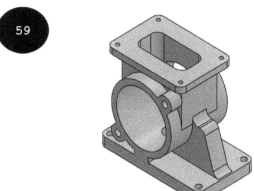

59

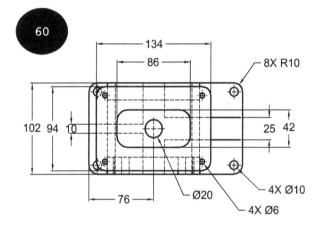

60

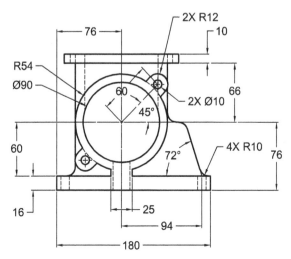

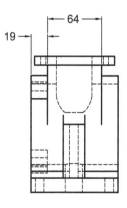

Exercise 31.

Create the 3D model shown in Figure 61. Different views of the model and dimensions are shown in Figure 62. All dimensions are in **mm**.   [Expected time: 30 min]

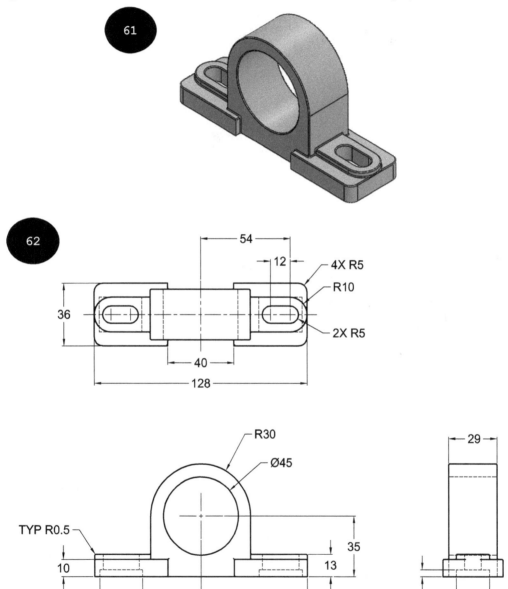

Exercise 32.

Create the 3D model shown in Figure 63. Different views of the model and dimensions are shown in Figure 64. All dimensions are in **mm**.   [Expected time: 30 min]

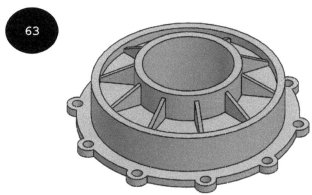

63

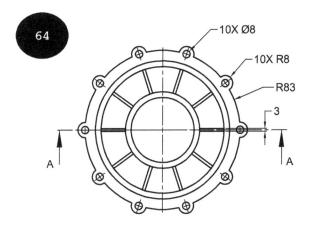

64

- 10X Ø8
- 10X R8
- R83
- 3

A   A

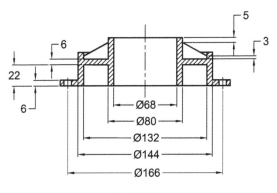

- 5
- 6
- 3
- 22
- 6
- Ø68
- Ø80
- Ø132
- Ø144
- Ø166

SECTION A-A

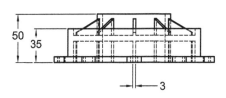

- 50
- 35
- 3

Exercise 33.

Create the 3D model shown in Figure 65. Different views of the model and dimensions are shown in Figure 66. All dimensions are in **mm**.   [Expected time: 30 min]

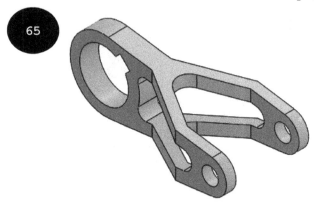

65

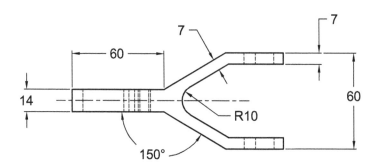

66

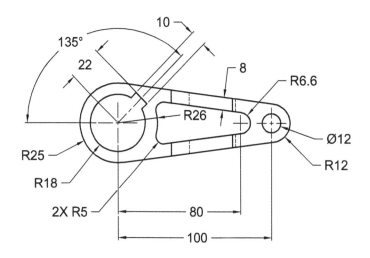

Exercise 34.

Create the 3D model shown in Figure 67. Different views of the model and dimensions are shown in Figure 68. All dimensions are in **mm**. [Expected time: 30 min]

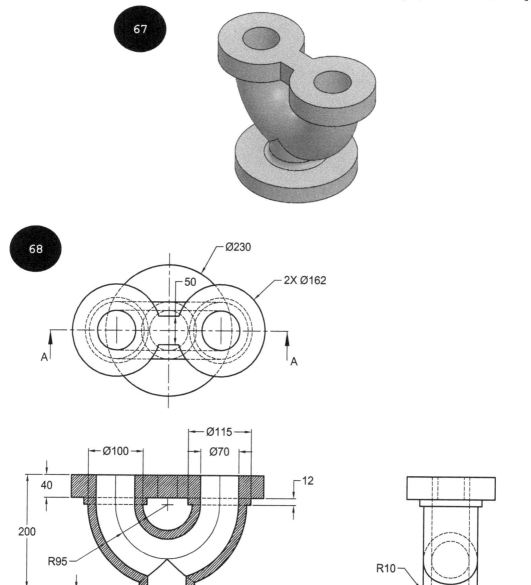

Exercise 35.

Create the 3D model shown in Figure 69. Different views of the model and dimensions are shown in Figure 70. All dimensions are in **mm**.   [Expected time: 30 min]

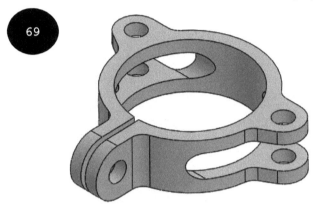

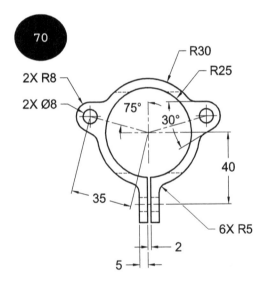

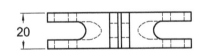

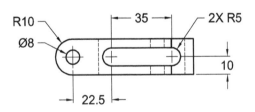

Exercise 36.

Create the 3D model shown in Figure 71. Different views of the model and dimensions are shown in Figure 72. All dimensions are in **mm**.   [Expected time: 30 min]

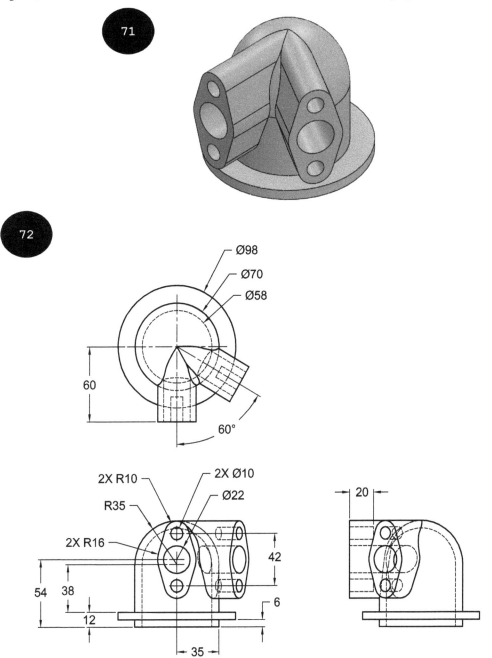

Exercise 37.

Create the 3D model shown in Figure 73. Different views of the model and dimensions are shown in Figure 74. All dimensions are in **mm**. [Expected time: 30 min]

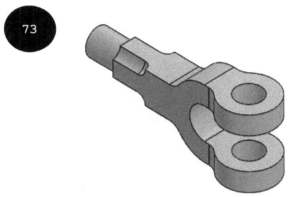

73

74

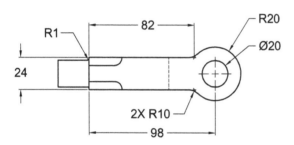

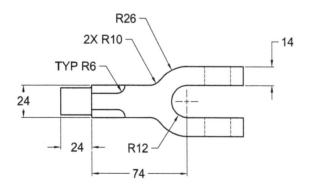

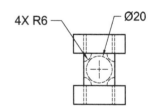

Exercise 38.

Create the 3D model shown in Figure 75. Different views of the model and dimensions are shown in Figure 76. All dimensions are in **mm**. [Expected time: 30 min]

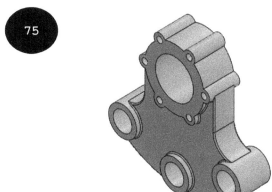

75

76

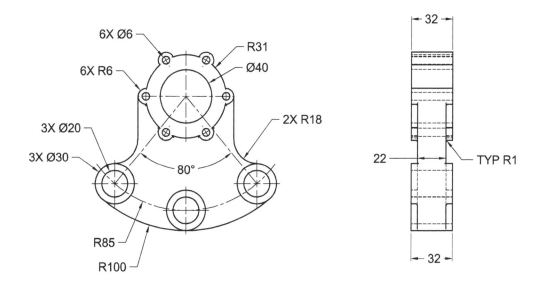

Exercise 39.

Create the 3D model shown in Figure 77. Different views of the model and dimensions are shown in Figure 78. All dimensions are in **mm**.   [Expected time: 30 min]

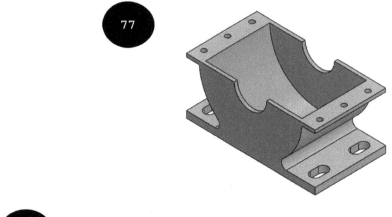

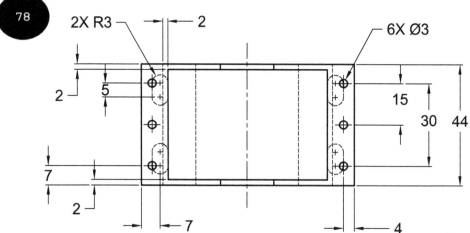

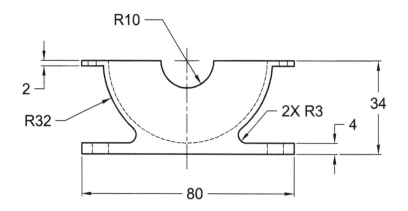

Exercise 40.

Create the 3D model shown in Figure 79. Different views of the model and dimensions are shown in Figure 80. All dimensions are in **mm**. [Expected time: 40 min]

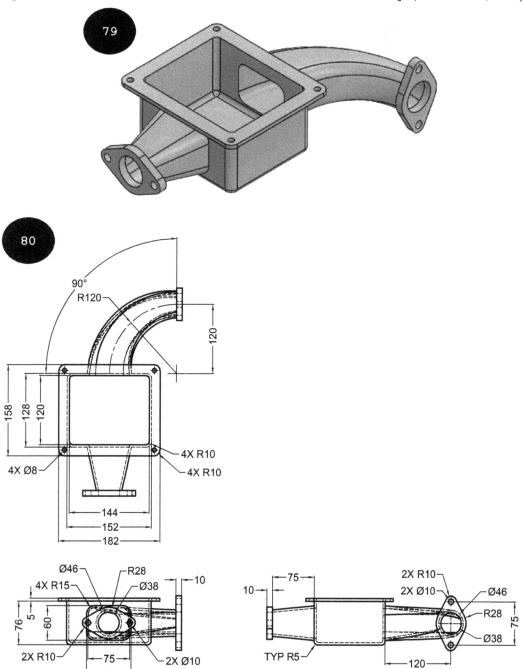

Exercise 41.

Create the 3D model shown in Figure 81. Different views of the model and dimensions are shown in Figure 82. All dimensions are in **mm**.   [Expected time: 30 min]

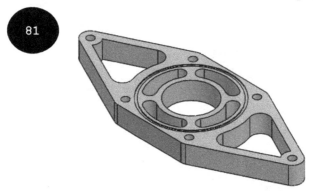

81

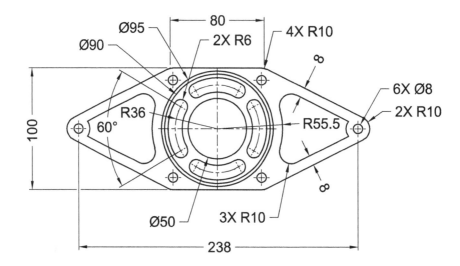

82

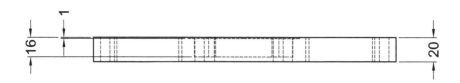

Exercise 42.

Create the 3D model shown in Figure 83. Different views of the model and dimensions are shown in Figure 84. All dimensions are in **mm**. [Expected time: 30 min]

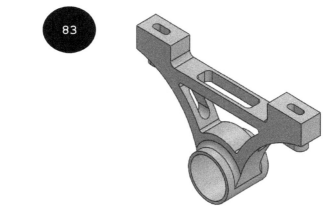

83

84

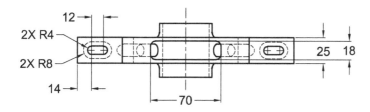

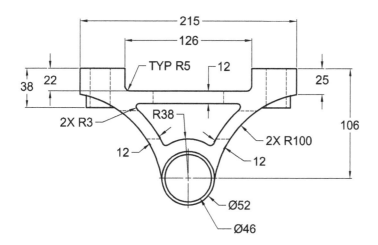

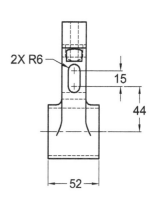

Exercise 43.

Create the 3D model shown in Figure 85. Different views of the model and dimensions are shown in Figure 86. All dimensions are in **mm**. [Expected time: 30 min]

85

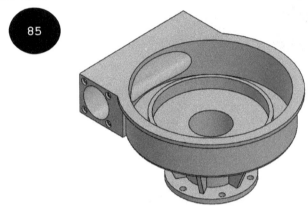

86

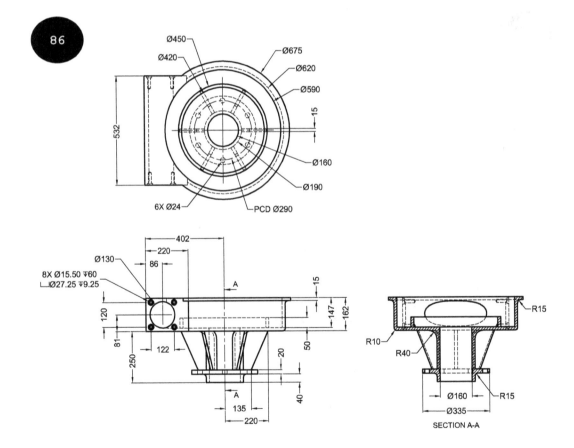

Exercise 44.

Create the 3D model shown in Figure 87. Different views of the model and dimensions are shown in Figure 88. All dimensions are in **mm**. [Expected time: 25 min]

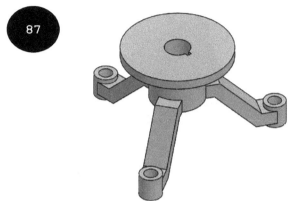

87

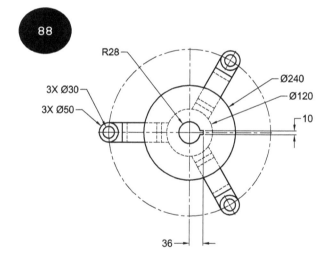

88

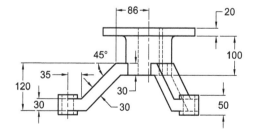

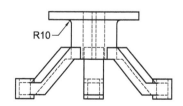

Exercise 45.

Create the 3D model shown in Figure 89. Different views of the model and dimensions are shown in Figure 90. All dimensions are in **mm**.   [Expected time: 30 min]

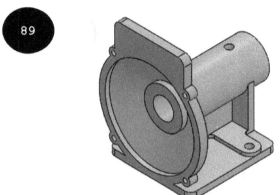

89

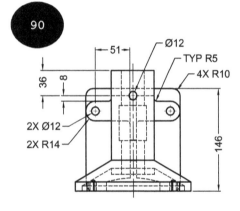

90

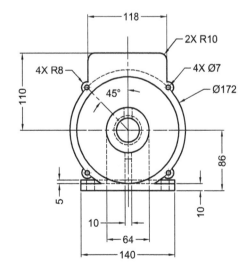

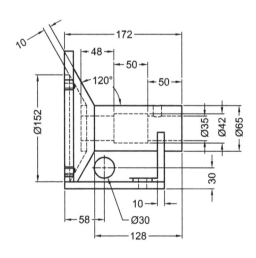

Exercise 46.

Create the 3D model shown in Figure 91. Different views of the model and dimensions are shown in Figure 92. All dimensions are in **mm**. [Expected time: 40 min]

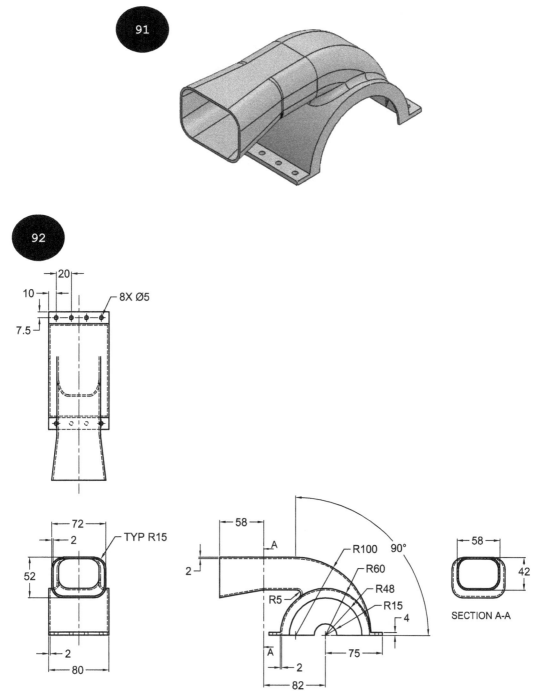

Exercise 47.

Create the 3D model shown in Figure 93. Different views of the model and dimensions are shown in Figure 94. All dimensions are in **mm**. [Expected time: 35 min]

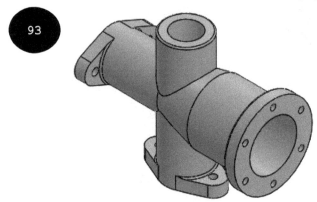

93

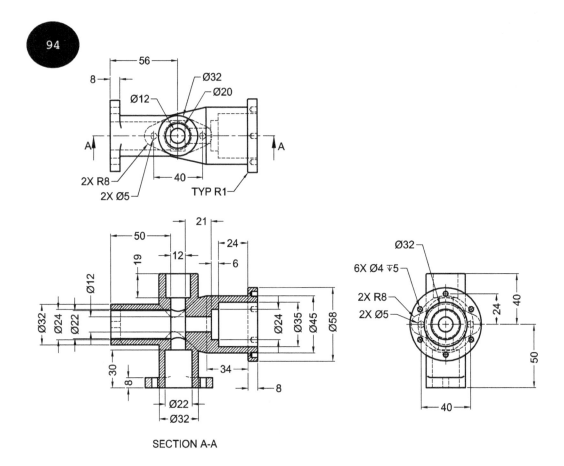

94

SECTION A-A

Exercise 48.

Create the 3D model shown in Figure 95. Different views of the model and dimensions are shown in Figure 96. All dimensions are in **mm**. [Expected time: 30 min]

95

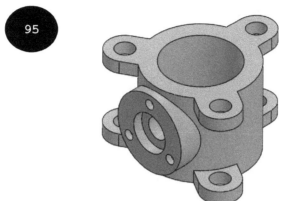

96

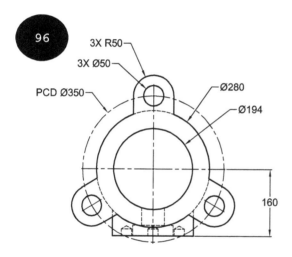

3X R50
3X Ø50
PCD Ø350
Ø280
Ø194
160

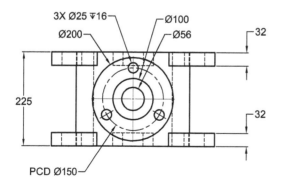

3X Ø25 ⊽16
Ø200
Ø100
Ø56
32
225
32
PCD Ø150

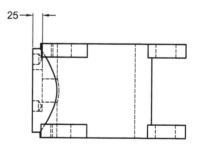

25

Exercise 49.

Create the assembly shown in Figure 97. The exploded view of the assembly is shown in Figure 98. Different views of the individual components of the assembly and dimensions are shown in Figures 99 and 100. All dimensions are in **mm**.   [Expected time: 1 hr. 20 min]

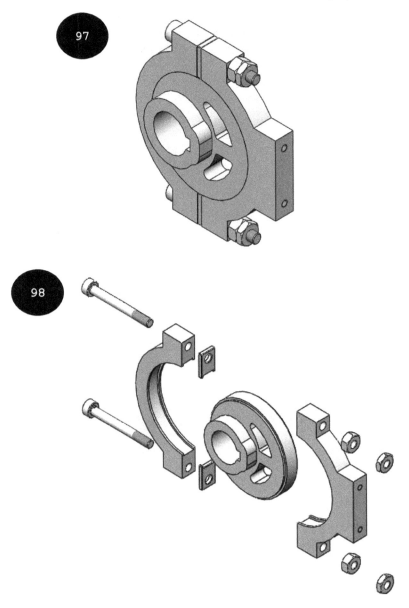

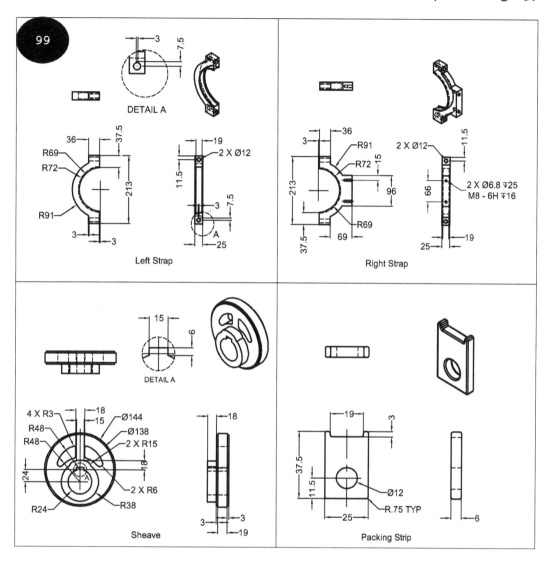

99

DETAIL A

Left Strap

Right Strap

DETAIL A

Sheave

Packing Strip

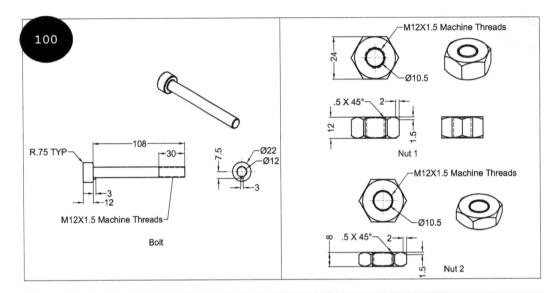

Exercise 50.

Create the assembly shown in Figure 101. The exploded view of the assembly is shown in Figure 102. Different views of the individual components of the assembly and dimensions are shown in Figures 103 and 104. All dimensions are in **mm**.   [Expected time: 1 hr. 20 min]

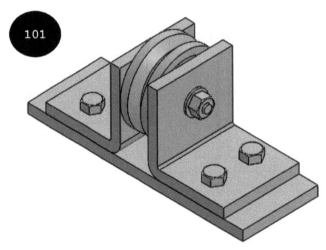

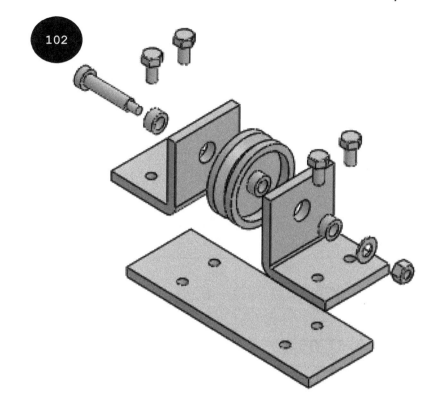

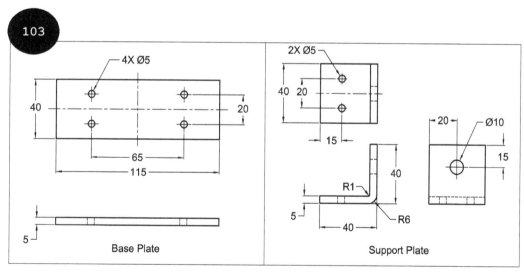

Base Plate

Support Plate

104

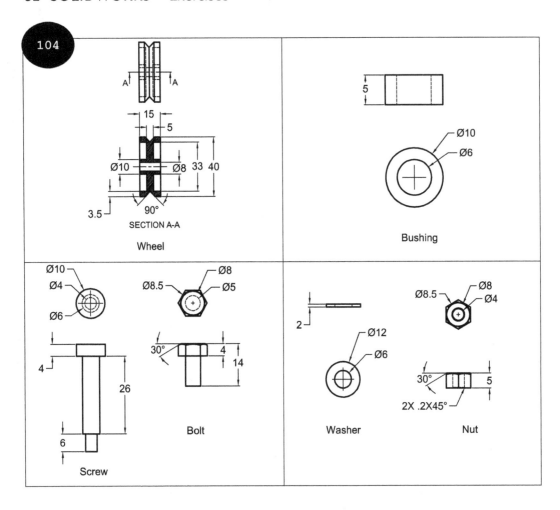

Wheel

SECTION A-A

Bushing

Screw

Bolt

Washer

Nut

www.ingramcontent.com/pod-product-compliance
Lightning Source LLC
Chambersburg PA
CBHW082112070326
40689CB00052B/4617